GW01608001

SBN 361 02129 1
© 1972 Walt Disney Productions
All Rights Reserved
Made and printed in Great Britain by
Purnell and Sons Limited, Paulton (Somerset) and London.

Rachel & sarah pearce.

WALT DISNEY'S

DISNEY ON PARADE

PURNELL
London

£1·00
In U.K. only

CONTENTS

DISNEY ON PARADE

DISNEY ON PARADE is a new, exciting, travelling show. It is the first time that Walt Disney's characters have appeared 'live' on stage in bright and colourful costumes.

It is a parade of over one hundred famous Disney characters, some larger than life, appearing together for the first time in one two-and-a-half-hour live stage musical show.

From the beginning, the people who thought up this idea decided that the show must be surrounded by an atmosphere of fantasy; everything must be exaggerated, colourful and imaginative. Because of the size of the arena, everything had to be larger than life; tap dancers had to leap into the air; costume-heads worn by the characters had to be three feet across; card characters had to be eight feet tall; and bird cages nine feet high.

At first the problem was how to

pack enough activity into the huge arena to hold everyone's interest for two and a half hours.

This was solved by blending magic with live production—films, sound effects, music and special lighting—so that cartoon characters are first introduced on a giant film screen in the form of a book, and then literally leap out into the arena to perform production numbers based on the classic stories.

All the time something is happening and the audience is encouraged to take part in the fun right from their seats.

The children become so involved with the characters that they scream advice at Snow White when she is offered the apple by the wicked witch. A tremendous cry of "Nooooo!" echoes round the arena. During one performance when Snow White took a bite out of the apple the arena was absolutely quiet. Then a desperate little voice called "Spit it out! Spit it out!"

As host of the show Mickey Mouse opens DISNEY ON PARADE when he makes a grand entrance with all his famous friends. Then, setting the atmosphere for the show, he plays again one of his most memorable film roles, the Sorcerer's Apprentice from 'Fantasia'. Creating a live cartoon Mickey performs a series of magic feats. He creates a bouquet of flowers from thin air; he makes a two-foot silver ball float in space and he highlights the sequence by making Pluto and four beautiful girls appear in the centre of the arena.

Daredevil trapeze artists sway on slender poles with head-spinning gyrations. They slide headfirst down the poles then stop inches from the ground in a heart-catching split second. A man rides on one wheel along a tightrope and, at the other end of the vast stage, two beautiful girls spin 20 feet in the air on a turning ladder, while the aerialists are now performing an 'iron jaw' routine, spinning high above the arena floor suspended only by their teeth. On the floor tumblers are turning cartwheels and bears are jumping through hoops. Cards march across the stage with military correctness and toy soldiers form fours and eights with the same degree of skill.

Dumbo puts a finishing touch to the routine. True to the original Walt Disney film, he flies high in the arena over his circus grand parade marching below.

Mickey's most spectacular performance comes when he rides a motorcycle on a high wire at the top of the arena balancing two beautiful girls. And to add to the excitement, all these high wire acts perform without a net to catch them should they fall.

Now the house lights dim, a pulsating rhythm of native drums from the depths of the darkness sets the beat, while the natural sounds of the jungle help create the mood for the production number from the 'Jungle Book'. While the drum beat builds up, an array of coloured lights suddenly flood the stage to reveal wild jungle scenes. Rock music, go-go dancers and psychedelic lighting accompany Baloo, King Louie and Mowgli who come to life, running wildly on the stage, while monkeys move through the audience and the dazzling go-go dancers perform. As the rock tempo builds with the action, lights flash on and off and everyone is caught up in the frantic rhythm.

The action constantly spills out among the audience and at the same time characters are appearing or disappearing in bright flashes of colour and sound.

One of the highlights of DISNEY ON PARADE is the live adaptation of 'Cinderella'. Unfolding on a storybook screen, the enchanting love story of the scullery maid who wins the heart of a handsome prince is first told with scenes from the classic cartoon feature, then becomes a dramatic stage presentation.

At this precise moment the entire arena is transformed into a palace and the audience sees a live musical production with masses of colourful dancers waltzing amid the glittering decorations for the Ball. Into this gorgeous setting, noisily and rudely, burst Cinderella's Stepmother and two ugly step-sisters who are, in reality, a speciality tumbling act. There follows a comedy knock-about act which

ends in the three of them falling down 18 steps to the dance floor.

The entire cast appears in 18th-century costumes to perform the minuet and waltz. There are nearly fifty expensively costumed dancers in this sequence and one dress worn by Cinderella was excessively costly considering she only wears it for one minute and thirty seconds!

The Alice in Wonderland production in DISNEY ON PARADE involves nearly the entire cast. The colourful sequence opens on a massive storybook screen where Alice and the story are introduced to the audience. The action suddenly leaps from the screen on to the arena stage where real live characters, led by Alice, pursue the White Rabbit through a floral Wonderland.

Where are they going? Why, to an un-birthday party, of course, with Tweedle Dum and Tweedle Dee, Walrus, March Hare and Dormouse in a sequence featuring motorised chairs and a 26-foot-wide mechanically operated un-birthday cake. What a party! Alice dances a beautiful ballet with dancing flowers, who turn into beautiful butterflies, gliding at tent top level in suffused lighting, their luminous wings making kaleidoscopic patterns in the air.

For the finale of the show, Mickey appears with the entire cast in a grand march, leading the audience in singing his famous song 'Mickey Mouse'. And to show how much the children have become involved in the show, when the costumed performers invite them to come down to the edge of the floor to say 'hello', there is a mad rush to 'touch' and to talk. The children know Mickey and his friends are their friends, so why should they be bashful?

MICKEY MOUSE

Mickey Mouse, Disney's first animated cartoon character, made his first appearance in 1928.

Today, Mickey appears as Master of Ceremonies in DISNEY ON PARADE. He is the most important character in the show, which brings to life all the Disney characters.

As.host, Mickey opens DISNEY ON PARADE when he makes a grand entrance with all of his friends. Then setting the atmosphere for the entire show, he re-creates one of his most memorable screen roles, that of the Sorcerer's Apprentice from 'Fantasia'.

In the following story, Mickey and Minnie decide to have a picnic with some friends without inviting Donald! Now read on.

MICKEY MOUSE'S PICNIC

MICKEY MOUSE sang:

"What a beautiful day for a picnic,
What a picnical day for a lark!
We will frolic all day
In the happiest way,
And we won't get back home
until dark!"

Mickey was feeling very happy as he skipped up the path to Minnie Mouse's house.

"Ready, Minnie?" he called.

Pluto, Goofy, Daisy Duck and Clarabelle Cow were waiting in Mickey's car.

"All ready," Minnie smiled. "I've packed us a nice big basket of lunch."

She let Mickey peep inside.

"Whee!" cried Mickey.

For Minnie had packed:

Peanut butter and jam sandwiches,
cold meat sandwiches,
devilled eggs, potato salad,
radishes, onions,
pink lemonade, and
a great big chocolate cake!

"Let's go!" said Mickey. And he picked up the basket and led Minnie out to the car.

"Let's go!" cried Goofy and Daisy and Clarabelle Cow.

"It seems strange to start off on a picnic without Donald Duck," said Mickey. "Don't you think maybe we should ask him anyway?"

"No!" said everyone.

"You remember last time, Mickey," Minnie Mouse reminded him. "We all decided not to take Donald on the next picnic. Because there is always trouble when Donald is around."

"Well, all right," Mickey said. "I guess we do have a car full anyway."

So Mickey hopped into the driver's seat. And away they went.

None of them saw a figure watching from behind the bushes. And when they were far down the road,

none of them saw that same figure come out from hiding and jump up and down in rage!

Everyone sang as Mickey Mouse drove merrily down the road to the picnic grounds.

"What a beautiful day for a picnic,
What a picnical day for a lark!"

And it did start out to be a perfect day. First they went for a walk along the river bank. They found a grassy spot beneath a tall, shady tree, and left Minnie's lunch basket there.

Then everyone went swimming in the old swimming pool. How good that fresh, cool water felt! They swam and floated, played around, and had a wonderful time.

"I'm hungry enough to eat that whole basketful of lunch myself," Mickey Mouse said after a while.

"We'll see that you don't, Mickey Mouse!" Minnie laughed. "But it is time to eat, I guess."

So they all scrambled out of the water and hurried off to dress.

"Say!" Goofy cried. "Look at this, will you!"

Goofy was holding up his pants. The legs were all tied into knots. So were his shirt sleeves. And Mickey's were, too.

"Some mischief maker must be around," Mickey said, with a shake of his head.

But Minnie had a worse thought than that.

"The lunch!" she cried. And she ran up to the shade of that old tree.

The lunch basket was gone!

"Oh!" groaned everyone. "Not the lunch!"

"Hurry into your clothes, everybody!" Mickey cried. "We'll soon find out about this."

They struggled to undo the knots in their clothes. Then they dressed in a flash and were off on the hunt.

All through the woods they hunted, under every bush and trailing vine. But not a sign of that lunch basket did they see.

At last they came out on the road

again, near where they had left Mickey's car. They were hot and tired and hungry and cross.

It was then that they met Donald Duck, walking along the road all by himself. He had a fishing pole over one shoulder. And a bundle hung from the end of the fishing pole.

Donald was whistling as he walked along, and he looked very pleased with himself.

"Well, hello!" he cried. "Imagine meeting you folks out here. I just came to do some fishing. Got tired of spending a lonely day at home."

"Oh—er—yes," said Mickey. He felt bad because they had left Donald behind.

"Where are you folks going?" Donald asked.

"We are hunting for our lunch," Mickey said.

"For lunch!" said Donald. "Why, I have enough for us all in my bundle here. I will be glad to share it with my friends."

Now everyone felt guilty. But they were hungry, so they said thank you, they would like to eat with Donald.

Under the same big shady tree Donald spread out his lunch.

It was delicious. There were:
Peanut butter and jam sandwiches,
cold meat sandwiches,
devilled eggs, potato salad,
radishes, onions,
pink lemonade, and

a great big chocolate cake!

A strange look came into Mickey and Minnie Mouse's eyes as they saw that picnic lunch. But they did not say a word.

So they all sat down and ate and ate.

"This is delicious, Donald," said Clarabelle Cow.

"And it is nice of you, too, Donald," Daisy Duck added, "to share it with us."

"Sure is," said Goofy.

"Yes," Mickey admitted. "I guess we misjudged you, Donald, old boy."

"Humph!" said Minnie Mouse. Then she turned to Donald with her sweetest smile.

"Did you bring a knife for cutting the chocolate cake, Donald?" she asked.

"Er—ah, I had one somewhere," Donald said. He looked all around. But he could not find it.

"I fastened a knife to the bottom of the cake stand with paper tape," Minnie said, "when I packed my picnic lunch today."

Mickey turned the cake stand upside down. And there, sure enough, was a knife, fastened to

D.O.P.—B

the bottom of the stand with paper tape. And on the knife handle were the letters M. M.

"Well!" said Mickey.

"Why, Donald!" cried Daisy Duck.

"So that's where our lunch disappeared to," cried Clarabelle Cow.

Donald dropped his eyes before their stony frowns. "I'm sorry, honest, I am," he said. "I won't ever do it again."

"And where is my lunch basket?" Minnie asked.

"In the back of Mickey's car," Donald admitted.

Everyone looked so solemn that Mickey had to laugh.

"Well," he said, as he cut the cake, and handed big slices around. "It was a good lunch anyway. And we've all learned a lesson, I think. Donald won't snatch any lunch baskets again, and we know it's better luck for a picnic to bring Donald along with us."

Everyone had to laugh then. And they all piled back into Mickey's car. They made room for Donald to sit in the empty lunch basket.

Then away they went toward town, singing merrily:

"We will frolic all day
In the happiest way,
And we won't get back home
until dark!"

THE THREE LITTLE PIGS AND BIG BAD WOLF

The 'Three Little Pigs' performance in DISNEY ON PARADE *is an adaptation of the 1934 film classic. The story has been updated for the show. Big Bad Wolf tries to outsmart the Three Little Pigs by threatening to 'Blow in your Pad'.*

However, our story is the original; for the new version you'll have to see the show.

THE THREE LITTLE PIGS

ONCE upon a time there were three little pigs who went out into the big world to build their homes and seek their fortunes.

The first little pig did not like to work at all. He quickly built himself a house of straw.

Then off he danced down the road, to see how his brothers were getting along.

The second little pig was building himself a house, too. He did not like to work any better than his brother, so he had decided to build a quick and easy house of sticks.

Soon it was finished, too. It was not a very strong little house, but at least the work was done. Now the second little pig was free to do what he liked.

What he liked to do was to play his fiddle and dance. So while the first little pig tooted his flute, the second little pig sawed away on his fiddle, dancing as he played.

And as he danced he sang:

"I built my house of sticks,
I built my house of twigs.
With a hey diddle-diddle
I play on my fiddle,
And dance all kinds of jigs."

Then off danced the two little pigs down the road together to see how their brother was getting along.

The third little pig was a sober little pig. He was building a house, too, but he was building his of bricks. He did not mind hard work, and he wanted a stout little, strong little house, for he knew that in the woods near by there lived a big bad wolf who liked nothing better than to catch little pigs and eat them up!

So slap, slosh, slap! Away he worked, laying bricks and smoothing mortar between them.

"Ha ha ha!" laughed the first little pig, when he saw his brother hard at work.

"Ho ho ho!" laughed the second little pig. "Come down and play with us!" he called.

But the busy little pig did not pause. Slap, slosh, slap! went bricks on mortar as he called down to them:

"I build my house of stones.
I build my house of bricks.
I have no chance

To sing and dance,
For work and play don't mix."

"Ho ho ho! Ha ha ha!" laughed the two lazy little pigs, dancing along to the tune of the fiddle and the flute.

"You can laugh and dance and sing," their busy brother called after them, "but I'll be safe and you'll be sorry when the wolf comes to the door!"

"Ha ha ha! Ho ho ho!" laughed the two little pigs again, and they disappeared into the woods singing a merry tune:

"Who's afraid of the big bad wolf,
The big bad wolf, the big bad wolf?
Who's afraid of the big bad wolf?
Tra la la la la-a-a-a!"

Just as the first pig reached his door, out of the woods popped the big bad wolf!

The little pig squealed with fright and slammed the door.

"Little pig, little pig, let me come in!" cried the wolf.

"Not by the hair of my chinny-chin-chin!" said the little pig.

"Then I'll huff and I'll puff, and I'll blow your house in!" cried the wolf.

But still the first little pig would not open his door.

So the big bad wolf huffed
and he PUFFED
and he *puffed*
and he HUFFED,
and he blew the little straw house all to pieces!

Away raced the little pig to the second little pig's house of sticks.

The second little pig had just time to let his brother in and bolt the door. Then, knock, knock, knock! There was the big bad wolf!

"Little pigs, little pigs, let me come in," said the wolf.

"Not by the hair of my chinny-chin-chin," said the second little pig.

"I'll fool them," chuckled the big bad wolf to himself. Then he said out loud, "Those little pigs are too smart for me. I'm going home."

He started off toward the deep woods, but he did not go far. Behind the big tree near the little pig's house he stopped and hid.

Soon the door opened and the two little pigs peeked out. There was no wolf in sight.

"Ha ha ha! Ho ho ho!" laughed the two little pigs. "We fooled him."

Then they danced around the room, singing gaily:

"Who's afraid of the big bad wolf,

The big bad wolf, the big bad wolf?
Who's afraid of the big bad wolf?
Tra la la la la-a-a-a!"

Soon there came another knock at the door. It was the big bad wolf again, but he had covered himself with a sheepskin, and was curled up in a big basket, looking like a little lamb.

"Who's there?" called the second little pig.

"I'm a poor little sheep, with no place to sleep. Please open the door and let me in," said the big bad wolf in a sweet little voice.

The little pig peeked through a crack of the door, and he could see the wolf's big black paws and sharp fangs.

"Not by the hair of my chinny-chin-chin!"

"You can't fool us!" said the second little pig. So the wolf leapt out of the sheepskin.

"Then I'll huff, and I'll puff, and I'll blow your house in!" cried the angry old wolf.

So he huffed
and he PUFFED
and he *puffed,*
and he HUFFED,
and he blew the little twig house all to pieces!

Away raced the two little pigs, straight to the third little pig's house of bricks.

"Don't worry," said the third little pig to his two frightened little brothers. "You are safe here."

Soon they were all singing gaily.

This made the big bad wolf perfectly furious!

"Now by the hair of my chinny-chin-chin," he roared, "I'll huff, and I'll puff, and I'll blow your house in!"

So the big bad wolf huffed,
and he PUFFED,
and he *puffed,*
and he HUFFED,
but he could not blow down that little house of bricks! How could he get in? At last he thought of the chimney!

So up he climbed, quietly. Then with a snarl, down he jumped—right into a kettle of boiling water!

With a yelp of pain he sprang straight up the chimney again, and raced away into the woods. The three little pigs never saw him again, and spent their time in the strong little brick house singing and dancing merrily.

DONALD DUCK

One star who has had more than his fair share of fan mail over the past thirty-five years is Donald Duck.

It all started when a bird and animal imitator gave his version of a scared little girl reciting 'Mary Had a Little Lamb'. Walt Disney heard it and said that it sounded like a duck talking. From that day in 1932 until today Donald Duck has not failed to make an audience laugh.

Donald Duck is constantly opposed in his attempts to recite a poem throughout the show. He fills in between acts with a polished performance of his own. His tail wags in anger each time the orchestra interrupts his recital.

Our story tells how Huey, Dewey and Louis fix a surprise for their Uncle Donald.

DONALD DUCK'S SURPRISE

"UNCA DONALD! Unca Donald! Can we have some more pocket money? We've spent all ours," cried Huey, Dewey and Louie.

"No! Definitely, positively, no, boys," said Donald. "You've had plenty."

"Aw, c'mon, don't be a meanie!"

"*No,* and I mean *no*! Go away and play," said Donald crossly.

"What shall we do now?" asked Huey.

"I've got an idea," said Dewey. "We'll cut the grass lawns for all our neighbours and make lots of money."

"Cut the grass?" asked Donald who had heard him. "What with?"

"Our special grass cutter!" said Huey.

"It has four legs, horns, a beard and a small tail!" cried the boys.

"Stop fooling," said Donald.

"No, look, there she is!" and the boys brought their goat for Donald to see.

"Oh, a goat! You always have trouble with goats," said Donald gloomily.

"Not *our* goat," cried the boys. "She's a fine, tame animal."

"Well, all right, then," said Donald, "but if there's any trouble, it's your fault!"

"Oh, there won't be. She's as good as gold!" said Huey, Dewey and Louie.

Off they went with their goat to plan how they could make the most money.

"Let's have a garden fête, with lots of games and things," said Huey.

"How?" asked Dewey.

"Easy. Here in this garden! We can make loads of dough here!"

"We must work it all out," said Louie. "Let's think what we can do."

And the nephews began to plan.

Next day, Huey, Louie and Dewey sat at the table hard at work. They were writing letters to all their friends, asking them to come to the garden fête.

They wrote and wrote, biting their pens and trying to spell very carefully.

"Shall we ask Unca Donald?" said Huey. "Do you think he'll come?"

"Of course he will," said Louie. "We must ask him. It's his garden."

"Oh, all right!"

Huey, Louie and Dewey had put their letters in the post. Now all they had to do was wait for the answers. Everyone had just *got* to come.

Unca Donald was up early. He walked down the garden, opened his mailbox and there was a letter for him! "I know this writing," he muttered, tearing it open. "But who is it from?"

"Dear Unca Donald," he read.

"We are giving a garden fête next week in your garden and we would like you to come. Please.

Huey, Dewey and Louie."

Those boys! They really meant business.

Trring, trring, the telephone rang.

"Donald, Donald, is that you?" cried a voice.

"Well, who do you expect it is?" asked Donald.

"Oh, Donald, be serious! It's Daisy!"

"Hullo, Daisy," said Donald. "How are you?"

"I'm going out of my mind!" screamed Daisy.

"Well, what's the matter with you?" asked Donald.

"Matter! There's a goat in my garden!" cried Daisy. "It's eating all my flowers."

"Uh, huh, goat trouble already," muttered Donald.

"What's that you say?" yelled Daisy. "Donald, *do* something!"

"I told you so," said Donald. "I told you it would mean trouble."

"Donald! Help!"

"O.K. Stay where you are," said Donald.

Donald hung up and walked over

to the window and looked out. What a sight met his eyes!

"Eeek!" Daisy was right. There was a goat in the garden. It was busily eating the best flowers, the red roses and the white daisies.

"Hey, goat!" Donald shouted, but it took no notice.

"Those wretched boys," Donald said. "I knew this would happen."

Where were those boys? There was no sign of them. He threw up the window. "Huey, Dewey and Louie," he shouted, "come here at once!"

There was no answer.

"Your goat's loose in the garden!" Donald yelled.

That fetched them. They came running up to the window.

"Unca Donald, Unca Donald, what's the matter?"

"The matter! It's your goat! It's loose in the garden and it's eating all the best flowers. Go and catch it at once!" he roared.

"Sure, sure," the boys cried and rushed out to catch the goat.

The goat sat down, eating a daisy, with a happy smile on her face.

"That goat must go!" shouted Donald. "I won't let it stay here another day!"

"Oh no, Unca Donald," cried the boys. "Please give her another chance!"

"No chance," said Donald. "That goat must go—the day after to-morrow, or I'll take her to the butcher."

With that he slammed down the window, and left Huey, Dewey and Louie to lead the goat away.

Things went from bad to worse. Next day, the goat escaped again. She saw a great pile of newspapers by the wall. "Oooh! Scrumptious!" She began to eat. She went on eating and eating until a furious man came along.

"You goat, you," he cried, "those are my newspapers! You've eaten all my papers."

But the goat just gave a little hiccough and looked at him.

"More trouble?" asked Donald

when he saw Huey, Dewey and Louie trying to pull a newspaper from the goat's mouth.

"That goat must go!" and he went indoors, shaking his head.

"Now listen, goat," cried the nephews, "you have got to behave. You have just got to be good. Promise!"

The goat hung her head as if she understood, and the boys went away.

Soon things began to happen again. The goat saw a barrow filled with lovely ripe bananas.

It was too much for her. She sat down beside them and ate the lot. All those beautiful yellow bananas were too good to miss.

"What can we do?" cried Huey, Dewey and Louie as they took her home. "Who would want a goat like that? We can just never sell her now. Everyone knows about her!"

They were very sad. There seemed no hope for their goat. Why couldn't she behave? Or why couldn't Unca Donald be reasonable?

"We must make plans," said Huey.

They sat down and thought hard.

"I have an idea," cried Dewey.

"An idea?" said Huey and Louie. "Tell us!"

Huey, Dewey and Louie sat on the steps of the house and thought about Dewey's idea. It was a good one, but they must keep it a secret.

The day of the garden fête was fine and warm. Huey, Dewey and Louie had worked hard to make the garden look nice. The goat had eaten the lawns which were smooth and shining, and the whole place was a mass of colour. The flowers bloomed, gay streamers were hung round the trees, coloured parasols, with little tables, stood round the lawn.

"Come on, everybody," cried

Huey, "come and have some food. There's lots of it!"

"Don't eat it all," muttered Dewey and Louie to themselves.

Everyone was there enjoying themselves.

The fête was a great success. There were lots of things to do. Games for the children, toffee-apples on a string to try and jump for, races to be run and other contests.

"Roll up! Roll up!" cried the boys. "Get your tickets for the grand raffle. Prizes for all!"

Everyone bought tickets for this exciting event. Who would win the first prize? And what would it be?

"I'll take six tickets," said Donald.

"Oh, thank you, Unca Donald," cried Huey. "I hope you win first prize."

"I hope so," said Donald.

"Ha ha!" laughed the boys.

"I'll have *one* ticket," said Daisy Duck. She hadn't forgotten the boys or the goat.

Everyone gathered round. It was time to draw the winning raffle ticket.

"Everybody quiet," yelled Huey. "Dewey is going to draw the prizes."

"Number 13, first prize," yelled Dewey.

"Who has it?" cried Louie.

"I do! I do! I do! It's mine!" cried Donald.

He was in such a hurry to get his prize that he sent all the other guests flying as he leapt to his feet, waving the winning ticket.

"The first raffle I've ever won," he panted as he reached the judges' table. "What is it?"

"Patience, patience," said Dewey. "The other two have gone to collect it."

Just as he said that Huey and Louie appeared with the goat. Somehow she looked different. She had been brushed and her hooves had been polished. In fact she looked very smart indeed.

"This is your prize, Unca Donald," the boys said.

"In fact," added Louie, "once she has been fully trained she'll save you money. She can keep your grass down and we all like goat's milk!"

They could see by the smile on Donald's face that they had won at last.

"O.K., boys," he said grudgingly, "you win. We can keep her in the garden provided she behaves herself and does no more damage."

"Oh, thank you, Unca Donald," they all said. But Donald didn't hear them, he was too busy stroking his goat!

CINDERELLA

One of the highlights of DISNEY ON PARADE is when Cinderella arrives at the ball in her beautiful gown and dances through forty gorgeously dressed couples with the handsome young Prince. She flees at the stroke of midnight, losing her slipper, and returns for her royal wedding.

But in order to know the whole story of Cinderella, read on.

CINDERELLA

Once upon a time in a far-off land, there lived a kindly gentleman. He had a fine home and a lovely little daughter, and he gave her all that money could buy—a horse of her own, a funny puppy dog, and beautiful dresses to wear.

But the little girl had no mother. She did wish for a mother and for other children to play with. So her father married a woman with two daughters. Now, with a new mother and sisters, he thought, his little daughter had everything to make her happy.

But alas! the kindly gentleman soon died. His fine home fell into disrepair. And his second wife was harsh and cold. She cared only for her own two ugly daughters. To her lovely stepdaughter she was cruel as cruel could be.

Everyone called the stepdaughter "Cinderella" now. For she had to work hard, she was dressed in rags, and she sat by the cinders to keep herself warm. Her horse grew old, locked up in the barn. And her dog was not allowed in the house.

But do you suppose Cinderella was sad? Not a bit! She made friends with the birds who flew to her window sill. She made friends with the barnyard chickens and geese. And her best friends of all were—guess who—the mice!

Every morning her friends the mice and birds woke Cinderella from her dreams. Then it was breakfast time for the household—with Cinderella doing all the work, of course.

Up the stairway she carried breakfast trays for her stepmother and her two lazy stepsisters. And down she came with a basket of mending, some clothes to wash, and a long list of jobs to do for the day.

One day the King himself gave orders to the Great Grand Duke. "The Prince must marry!" said the King. "It is high time!"

"But, Your Majesty, what can we do?" asked the duke. "First he must fall in love."

"We can arrange that," said the King. "We shall give a great ball, this very night, and invite every girl in the land!"

There was great excitement in Cinderella's home when the invitations to the King's ball came.

"How delightful!" the stepsisters said to each other. "We are going to the palace to a ball!"

"And I—" said Cinderella, "I am invited too!"

"Oh, you!" laughed the stepsisters.

"Yes, you!" mocked the stepmother. "Of course you may go, if you finish your work," she said. "And if you have something suitable to wear."

Cinderella worked as hard as she could, all the long day. But when it was time to leave for the ball, she had not had a moment to fix herself up, or to give a thought to a dress.

"Why, Cinderella, you are not ready," said her stepmother, when the coach was at the door.

"No. I am not going," said Cinderella sadly.

"Not going! Oh, what a shame!" the stepmother said with her mocking smile.

Poor Cinderella! She went to her room and sank sadly down, with her head in her hands.

Her little friends had not forgotten her. They had been scampering and flying about, as busy as could be, fixing a party dress for her to wear.

"Oh, how lovely!" she cried. "I can't thank you enough," she told all the birds and the mice. She looked out the window. The coach was still there. So she started to dress for the ball.

"Wait!" cried Cinderella. "I am coming too!"

She ran down the long stairway just as the stepmother was giving her daughters some last commands. They turned and stared.

"My beads!" cried one stepsister.

"And my ribbon!" cried the other, snatching off Cinderella's sash. "And those bows! You thief! Those are mine!"

So they pulled and they ripped and they tore at the dress, until Cinderella was in rags once more.

Poor Cinderella! She ran to the garden behind the house, and there she sank down on a low stone bench and wept as if her heart would break.

But soon she felt someone beside her. She looked up, and through her tears she saw a sweet-faced woman.

"I am your fairy godmother," said the little woman. And from the thin air she pulled a magic wand. "Now dry your tears. You can't go to the ball looking like that!

"Let's see now, the first thing you will need is—a pumpkin!" the fairy godmother went on.

Cinderella did not understand, but she brought the pumpkin.

"And now for the magic words! Salaga doola, menchika boola–bibbidi, bobbidi, boo!"

Slowly, the pumpkin turned into a handsome magic coach.

"What we need next is some fine big–mice!"

Cinderella brought her friends the mice. And at the touch of the wand they turned into prancing horses.

Then the old horse became a fine coachman.

And Bruno the dog turned into a footman at the touch of the wand and a "Bibbidi, bobbidi, boo!"

"There," said the fairy godmother, "now hop in, child. You've no time to waste. The magic only lasts till midnight! You'd better go."

"But my dress—" Cinderella looked at her rags.

"Good heavens, child!" laughed the fairy godmother. "Of course you can't go in that! Bibbidi, bobbidi, boo!"

The wand waved again, and there stood Cinderella in the most beautiful gown in the world, with tiny slippers of glass.

The Prince's ball had started. The palace was blazing with lights. The ballroom gleamed with silks and jewels. And the Prince smiled and bowed, but still looked bored, as all the young ladies of the kingdom in turn curtsied before him.

Up above on a balcony stood the King and the Duke, looking on. "Whatever is the matter with the

Prince?" cried the King. "He doesn't seem to care for one of those beautiful maidens."

"I feared as much," the Duke said with a sigh. "The Prince is not one to fall in love at first sight."

But just at that moment he did! For at that moment Cinderella appeared at the doorway of the ballroom. The Prince caught sight of her through the crowd. And like one in a dream he walked to her side and offered her his arm.

Quickly the King beckoned to the musicians, and they struck up a dreamy waltz. The Prince and Cinderella swirled off in the dance.

All evening the Prince never left Cinderella's side. They danced every dance. They ate supper together. And Cinderella had such a wonderful time that she quite forgot the fairy godmother's warning until the clock in the palace tower began to strike midnight.

"Oh!" cried Cinderella. The magic was about to end!

Without a word she ran from the ballroom, down the long palace hall, and out the door. One of her little glass slippers flew off, but she could not stop.

She leaped into her coach, and away they raced for home. But as they rounded the first corner the clock finished its strokes. The spell was broken. And there in the street stood an old horse, a dog, and a ragged girl, staring at a small round pumpkin. About them some mice ran chattering noisily.

"Glass slipper!" the mice cried.

And Cinderella looked down. Sure enough, there was a glass slipper on the pavement.

"Oh, thank you, godmother!" she said.

Next morning there was great excitement in the palace. The King was furious when he found that the Duke had let the beautiful girl slip away.

"All we could find was this one glass slipper," the Duke admitted. "And now the Prince says he must marry the girl whom this slipper fits. And he will not marry anyone else."

"He did?" cried the King. "He said he would marry her? Well then, find her! Scour the kingdom, but find that girl!"

All day and all night the Grand Duke with his servant travelled about the kingdom, trying to find a foot on which the glass slipper would fit. In the morning, his coach drove up before Cinderella's house.

The news of the search had run on ahead, and the stepmother was busy rousing her ugly daughters and preparing them to greet the Duke. For she was determined that one of them should wear the slipper and be the Prince's bride.

"The Prince's bride!" whispered Cinderella. "I must dress, too."

Cinderella went off to her room to dress, humming a waltzing tune. Then the stepmother suspected the truth—that Cinderella was the girl the Prince was seeking—and would marry! So the stepmother followed Cinderella—to lock her in her room.

Then Cinderella heard the key click. The door was locked.

"Please let me out—oh, please!" she cried. But the wicked stepmother only laughed and left.

"We will save you!" said the mice.

The Grand Duke had arrived. His servant held the glass slipper.

"It is mine!" "It is mine!" both stepsisters cried.

And each strained and pushed and tried to force her foot into the tiny glass slipper. But they failed.

Meanwhile, the mice had made themselves into a long, live chain. The mouse at the end dropped down into the stepmother's pocket. He popped up again with the key to Cinderella's room!

Now the Grand Duke was at the door, about to leave. Suddenly, down the stairs came Cinderella.

"Oh, wait, wait, please!" she called. "May I try the slipper on?"

"Of course," said the Duke. And he called back the servant with the slipper. But the wicked stepmother tripped the boy. Away sailed the slipper, and crash! it splintered into a thousand pieces. "Oh my, oh my!" said the Duke. "What can I ever tell the King?"

"Never mind," said Cinderella. "I have the other here." And she pulled it from her pocket.

So off to the palace went Cinderella in the King's own coach, with the happy Grand Duke by her side. The Prince was delighted to see her again. And so was his father, the king. So was everyone.

In no time at all she was Princess of the land. And she and her husband, the charming Prince, rode to their palace in a golden coach to live Happily Ever After!

JOIN THE DOTS

JUNGLE BOOK

Rudyard Kipling's Jungle Book characters have come to life in a bright, colourful, exciting way in DISNEY ON PARADE.

Our next story tells how Mowgli meets Baloo, and his adventures as a 'man-cub' in the jungle.

THE JUNGLE BOOK

BALOO THE BEAR came down the forest trail one bright and beautiful day.

Baloo rounded a turn in the path and stopped and blinked. "Well," said he, "what have we here?"

The small boy who sat scratching at the ground with a twig did not even look up.

"I believe it's a man-cub!" said Baloo. He bent and sniffed at the boy in a friendly fashion.

"You leave me alone!" cried the man-cub. He got up and aimed a puny punch at Baloo's midsection.

"Pitiful!" said Baloo. "Boy, you need help. Want old Baloo to teach you to fight like a bear?"

The boy stopped scowling. His big dark eyes grew wide. "Would you?" he asked.

"Sure. First, growl. Scare me."

The man-cub bared his teeth and growled. As growls went in that part of the woods, it amounted to nothing at all.

"Um!" said Baloo. He didn't want to hurt the man-cub's feelings. "We could try a little footwork," he suggested brightly.

The man-cub clenched his fists and danced back and forth in front of Baloo. He darted in under the bear's arms and punched. He missed. Baloo swung a huge paw and the man-cub went sprawling.

"Fine teacher you are," said a chilly voice.

The bear looked around. Bagheera, the prim and proper black panther, sat watching. "Tell me," said Bagheera, "if you knock your pupil senseless, how do you expect him to remember the lesson?"

Baloo frowned. He was not fond of Bagheera. The panther was forever asking awkward questions.

The man-cub scrambled to his feet. "I'm not hurt," he insisted. "I'm tough!"

"You're all right, boy," said Baloo. "Say, what do they call you?"

"He is Mowgli," said Bagheera.

"Mowgli?" Baloo cocked his head to one side and looked at the man-cub with real interest. He had, of course, heard of Mowgli. All the jungle animals knew his story. Mowgli was the human baby who had been found abandoned beside a stream. The wolf pack had adopted him and raised him as their own.

"I'm taking him to the man-village," said Bagheera. "The wolf pack has decided that he must return to his own people."

Baloo was horrified. "But they'll ruin him. They'll make a man out of him!"

"I want to stay in the jungle," Mowgli protested.

"Of course you do," said Baloo.

"And just how would he survive in the jungle?" asked stuffy old Bagheera.

It was another of those awkward questions, but this time Baloo was ready. A wonderful idea had bloomed in his mind. He would adopt Mowgli. The man-cub would make a great bear. "I'll take care of him," said Baloo. "I'll teach him all I know."

"That shouldn't take long," snorted Bagheera.

Baloo wasn't listening. Nor was Mowgli. First, said Baloo, Mowgli was not to worry. In the jungle, there was nothing to worry about. Coconuts and bananas and pawpaws grew everywhere. Bees hummed on every side, making honey just for the jungle folk. And one could always pick up a handful of tasty ants.

Mowgli wasn't sure about the ants, but he was fond of bananas and pawpaws and honey. "I'm going to like being a bear," he said.

"You bet you are," Baloo agreed. "This is really the life." He let his legs fold under him so that he slid down a little bank into a river that flowed slowly past.

Mowgli slid into the river, too. It felt good.

Baloo scooped Mowgli out of the water and set the man-cub high and dry on his furry stomach. The two floated peacefully along.

Then, so quickly that Baloo did not even see it happen, Mowgli disappeared.

"Baloo!" The scream came from high overhead.

Baloo splashed out of the stream. He looked up and he felt himself go cold. A band of chattering, gibbering monkeys had snatched Mowgli.

"Give me back my man-cub!" yelled Baloo.

"Come and get him!" jeered one of the monkeys, and he pelted Baloo with fruit.

"Baloo! Help me!" cried Mowgli.

"What happened?" Bagheera the panther had heard the man-cub scream and had come running along the river bank. "Where's Mowgli?"

"Those mangy monkeys," said Baloo miserably. "They carried him off."

"Hah!" said the panther. "Well, don't just sit there. We have to get the man-cub back!"

Baloo looked up into the green and empty treetops. "How do we do that?" he wondered.

Bagheera thought about it for a moment. "They'll take him to their king," he said. "They'll take him to those old ruins."

"The hidden city?" said Baloo. "But we never go there."

"We'd better go now if we want to see Mowgli again," said Bagheera.

The two animals set out toward the forbidden place where once men had piled stones upon stones to make palaces and temples. Long ago the men had left the city.

No respectable animal ever went to the ruined city. But the Ape King, who was more than a little mad, held his court there. He ruled his empty-headed band of monkeys from a man-thing called a throne.

Baloo looked through the gap in the wall. He saw the Ape King crouched on his throne. He saw the glittering eyes of hundreds of monkeys.

And he saw Mowgli.

"I hear that you want to stay in the jungle," said the Ape King.

"Yes," answered Mowgli.

"Well, I can fix it for you," offered the Ape King. "We're cousins, after all. I walk like you. I talk like you. I want to be a man, man-cub. All I need is the secret. Tell me how to make the red flower."

"The *red* flower? *Fire?* But I don't know how to make fire."

Baloo was shocked. Every right-thinking animal feared man's fire.

"We must be quick," said Bagheera. "Baloo, you create a disturbance, and I'll rescue Mowgli."

Just then, the Apes began to croon and dance, and Baloo was hypnotised by the beat.

And he *was* gone, right through

the break in the wall. "Oh no!" moaned Bagheera as the bear joined the dancing monkeys and stamped and swayed to their music.

The Ape King looked around. At first he thought he had a very large ape among his subjects. Then he looked more closely.

"Baloo!" shouted the Ape King.

"Baloo!" cried Mowgli. "It's you!"

Baloo seized Mowgli and ran. Unfortunately, the bear had no time to plot a course. Instead of making for the gap in the stone wall, he dodged down into one of the dark corridors of the old palace.

"After him!" shrieked the Ape King.

The Ape King darted in from one side and Mowgli was snatched away from Baloo.

"Give me my man-cub!" snarled Baloo. He lumbered after the ape, and brushed against a huge pillar. Stones rumbled and slid.

"My city!" yelped the Ape King.

The Ape King dropped Mowgli, and Baloo picked up the man-cub.

A wall buckled and came crashing down.

Bagheera was beside Baloo. "This way!" he said.

The bear, the panther, and the man-cub raced out through the shattered wall. They ran into the cool jungle night. They did not stop until the cries of the monkeys had faded behind them.

Mowgli slept that night beneath a huge tree, and Bagheera and Baloo kept watch. The bear dozed from time to time, but just before dawn, the panther roused him.

"What is it?" asked the bear.

"Baloo, you can't adopt Mowgli," said Bagheera. "He has to go back to the man-village."

"Oh, stop worrying, Bagheera," said the bear. "I'll take care of him."

"You can't," said Bagheera. "Shere Khan the tiger is returning to this part of the jungle. The ravens brought news of it two days ago. That's why the wolf pack sent Mowgli away."

"Shere Khan?" Baloo was puzzled. "What's he got to do with Mowgli?"

"He hates man with a vengeance. You know that. He fears man's gun and man's fire."

"But Mowgli doesn't have a gun, or fire."

"Shere Khan won't wait until he

does," said the panther wisely.

Baloo looked at the panther in silent misery. He knew Bagheera was right.

"You must do what's best for the boy," said Bagheera. "Make Mowgli go to the man-village."

"Wake Mowgli now and tell him," urged Bagheera.

Baloo shivered and sighed, but he did wake Mowgli. And told him.

"But you said I could be a bear!" cried Mowgli. "You're just like Bagheera!" Mowgli turned and disappeared into the underbrush.

Again the bear and the panther joined forces to hunt for the man-cub. They followed Mowgli's scent through the jungle.

"I'll take to the trees," said Bagheera. "Maybe I can spot him from there. You search the riverbank.

Bagheera darted up a tree trunk while Baloo nosed along the bank. Sure enough, not a mile had the bear gone before he found the footprints. But this time Baloo saw a second set of tracks. A giant cat had come this way, following close behind the man-cub. Shere Khan was on Mowgli's trail!

The sky darkened as Baloo forced his way through dense thickets. Mowgli must have raced in panic; his heels had dug hard into the earth of the jungle floor.

Purple-black storm clouds hung low in the sky when Baloo came to a place where the jungle ended and a barren plain stretched ahead. Beside a black pool stood a blasted, lifeless tree. Mowgli was there, facing his enemy, Shere Khan.

"Run, Mowgli!" yelled Baloo, and the bear threw himself forward and caught the tiger by the tail.

Shere Khan gasped and roared with rage. His great paw went up.

At that instant there was a deafening clap of thunder. Lightning split the sky and darted down to sear the shrivelled tree stump. The tiger struck, and pain exploded in Baloo's head.

The bear knew nothing for a time. Then he knew that he was lying on the ground and his head hurt very badly. And it was raining.

"Bagheera?" Mowgli spoke softly. "Bagheera, what's the matter with Baloo?"

The man-cub was alive. Baloo felt a great joy. Still, he was not quite ready to open his eyes.

"You must be brave," said Bagheera the panther. "You must be as brave as Baloo was."

"Oh, Bagheera!" cried Mowgli.

"When great deeds are remembered in this jungle, one name will stand above all others," said the panther. "The name of our friend, Baloo the bear."

Baloo opened one eye and peeked. Mowgli knelt beside him. Tears and rain were running down his face. Bagheera sat like a solemn statue. "This spot where Baloo fell will be a hallowed place," he said.

Baloo opened both his eyes and chuckled his deepest chuckle. "Don't stop, Baggy," he coaxed. "You're doing great!"

"You four-flusher!" scolded Bagheera.

"Baloo! Baloo, you're alive!" Mowgli hurled himself at the bear. "You're all right!"

"Never felt better." This was not quite true. Baloo sat up stiffly and rubbed his head. "What happened to old stripes?" he wanted to know.

"Shere Khan?" said Bagheera. "Mowgli drove him away."

"Is that the truth? Say, boy, you're really all right!"

"Mowgli is a man, after all," said Bagheera. "He used man's weapon." The panther nodded toward the tree stump. It sizzled in the rain and wisps of smoke curled up from it. "Lightning struck that dead tree," said Bagheera. "The red flower bloomed there. Mowgli took a blazing branch and the tiger fled. I saw it. Shere Khan will never come back to this part of the jungle."

"That's my boy!" laughed Baloo. He gave the man-cub a big bear hug.

"Now I can stay with you, Baloo," said Mowgli.

"You bet you can," said Baloo.

Bagheera looked pained. He was a most orderly panther, and he liked things in their proper places. Surely the man-village was the proper place for a man-cub. However, Mowgli had defeated the dreaded Shere Khan. Bagheera could argue no more.

"The man-cub has earned the right to stay," admitted Bagheera. A crafty look stole across the panther's face. "It seems rather a shame," said he. "We've come very close to the man-village. Would you like to see it, Mowgli?"

"It's quite interesting," said Bagheera. "We won't go in, of course, or show ourselves in any way. We can just look from the edge of the jungle."

"Well," said Mowgli, "as long as we don't go in."

He and Baloo followed Bagheera back into the jungle and along a trail to a place where a brook bubbled over some stones and splashed into a clear little pool. And beyond the meadow was a fence made of stakes. Mowgli saw thatched roofs inside the fence. Smoke drifted up. "The red flower blooms in the man-village," said Mowgli.

"Always," replied Bagheera.

A gate in the fence swung open, and a little girl came out and walked across the meadow. She had a jug balanced on her head.

"What's that?" asked Mowgli.

"It's a girl-cub," said Bagheera quietly.

"Forget about those," warned Baloo. "They're nothing but trouble."

"I want a better look," said

Mowgli. He shinned up a tree that grew next to the pool.

The girl-cub reached the pool and bent to fill her jug. Mowgli edged out on to a branch to get a better view. There was a brisk crack. The branch split and Mowgli tumbled down into the pool.

The little girl was not a bit upset. She giggled. Mowgli got up and took a step or two toward her —whereupon she dropped the jug.

"Don't do it," breathed Baloo.

But Mowgli did it. He picked up the jug and held it out to the girl-cub. She did not take it. Instead, she turned and walked back toward the man-village. After a short, bewildered moment, Mowgli put the jug on his own head and walked after her. At the village gate he paused. Then he followed the girl.

"It had to happen, Baloo," said Bagheera. "Mowgli is among his own people, where he belongs."

The panther and the bear turned from the man-village. Poor Baloo felt completely bereft. But it was not possible for the bear to grieve for very long. The sun had come out and it was warm in the clearings. Baloo began to sing of pawpaw trees and mangoes and other things dear to the heart of a bear. But when he and Bagheera came to a fork in the trail, and the panther stopped to take his leave, Baloo made a last protest.

"I still think he'd have made one swell bear!" said Baloo.

The panther nodded. "He would have made a most admirable bear."

A PICTURE TO COLOUR

PLUTO

The World's best known hound, Pluto, appears in DISNEY ON PARADE with twenty trained dogs to defeat a bumbling dog catcher.

Pluto, long and gangling, with an itchy-looking yellow coat, skinny neck and long swinging ears, helpless in trouble, this time comes out on top. The fun starts when the dog catcher drives his van on to the stage and catches sight of Pluto. Pluto avoids the dog catcher's net, releases his small friends from the van—and the dog antics begin!

His devotion to Mickey and his utter helplessness in disastrous situations make him a really lovable character.

In the following story, Uncle Scrooge Duck needs to borrow Pluto from Mickey—and the reason? He needs a hunting dog!

PLUTO GOES HUNTING

ONE SUNNY day Scrooge McDuck decided to go hunting. A great idea! But there was one snag. He had no hunting dog! What could he do? He thought and thought, and then he had a fine idea. He would borrow Pluto! He was sure Mickey wouldn't mind. He would ring him up right away.

"Hello, Mickey," he said. "Scrooge here."

"Oh, hello, Uncle Scrooge. How are you?"

"Fine, just fine. But I have a little problem."

"A problem? Can I help?" Mickey asked.

"Yes, boy, I think you can. I planned on going hunting tomorrow, but I don't have a hunting dog."

"No dog?" asked Mickey puzzled. "But how can I help?"

"Well, I was just wondering. How about Pluto coming along?"

"Pluto?" echoed Mickey. "He hasn't actually done much hunting, but I'm sure he would pick it up very quickly. I'll ask him."

Mickey turned and called Pluto. "Pluto, Uncle Scrooge wants to know if you would like to go hunting with him tomorrow?"

"Woof! Woof! Wouldn't I!" Pluto barked.

"Yes, Uncle Scrooge, he says he would like it very much."

"Marvellous! You've just saved my bacon, old boy," said Scrooge.

Next morning, very early, before Mickey had finished his breakfast, Uncle Scrooge arrived on his doorstep.

"Come on, Mickey! It's time to get up," called Uncle Scrooge.

"Coming, coming," called Mickey.

"I'm so excited about my hunting trip, I couldn't sleep last night," said Uncle Scrooge. "Now, where's that hound dog? Pluto!"

With a bound that nearly sent Uncle Scrooge flying, Pluto appeared.

"Pluto is all ready," smiled Mickey. "He's so keen to go."

Pluto began to bark excitedly, and they rushed out to the car.

Uncle Scrooge slammed the door and started the car. He put his foot down hard and they were off.

"Good hunting!" called Mickey from the doorstep.

It was a lovely day and the car sped along. Uncle Scrooge began to sing in a rough voice. "Ho, ho, ho, a huntin' we will go!"

Very soon they came to the edge of the woods and Uncle Scrooge stopped the car and got out. Pluto leaped to the ground and began sniffing round excitedly.

"Wait a minute, Pluto," said Uncle Scrooge. "Let me get my gun out!"

But Pluto was off like a flash! What a wonderful place this was! He ran around barking, looking here and there. Uncle Scrooge called and called him. "Wait for me, Pluto! What's the rush?"

With a joyous bark, Pluto set off in pursuit of a hare. It ran faster than he could, and he stared after it with a disappointed face.

Ah, this looked better. A furry, bushy-tailed animal. He would soon catch him. Pluto raced after the red squirrel, who, clapping his paws together and chattering excitedly, soon scrambled up a tree. "Take that, you hound," he called, throwing nuts at Pluto, who stood barking underneath.

A huge bird with a fine, long, long tail was pecking the ground nearby. "Aha," Pluto thought, "I will catch this fine pheasant."

Pluto charged. His tail flew up in the air and his ears stood on end. He would show them! He barked.

The bird rose up in the air, just as he reached it, with a flutter of wings. Then it was gone. There was only a speck on the skyline.

"Missed again," muttered Pluto. Then he heard Uncle Scrooge calling.

"Pluto! Pluto! Come back here at once," he called. "What do you think you are playing at? Come back here, right now."

Pluto could not understand it at all. He returned to Uncle Scrooge, thinking he might be able to tell him where all the animals had gone.

Uncle Scrooge was very cross, but when he saw how sad Pluto was looking he decided to explain things to him.

"Now, listen here, old boy," he said. "I guess I'll have to show you

just how to hunt. You don't *chase* the animals, you creep up quietly behind them and then surprise them."

"You don't run after them?" barked Pluto in surprise.

"No, no. The plan is to come up on them quietly and make sure they don't hear you."

Pluto wagged his tail, he understood.

"Right, then, let's try again," said Uncle Scrooge, and they set off down the woodland trail.

Pluto tried to be very good. He crawled along on all fours very quietly. He looked this way and that, sniffing, very slowly, very carefully.

He was tracking! It was all very interesting, but he kept getting soil in his mouth and up his nose. Suddenly he lifted his head. He stood quite still. He had found something! There it was, just in front of him, a large, long-tailed pheasant.

"Oh, lovely," thought Pluto. "Pheasant for dinner. I like pheasant."

Uncle Scrooge had seen it too. He took out his gun, loaded it, aimed and fired. *Bang!* went the

gun, but the shot missed. The pheasant flew away, out of sight.

"Bother, bother, bother!" said Uncle Scrooge.

How did it happen? Did Uncle Scrooge miss? No, not at all. He is a fine shot.

Just as Uncle Scrooge was taking aim Pluto dashed up and knocked his arm. He wanted that pheasant himself!

"Oh dear! You silly hound! Now he has gone and there are no more," said Uncle Scrooge sadly. "What a day!"

Pluto barked at him.

"Yes, it's all your fault. Of all the hounds to borrow, I have to have one which is enough to make a man weep!"

Poor, poor Pluto! Whatever he tried to do went wrong. And he tried so hard too!

"I'm sorry," Pluto barked sadly.

But Uncle Scrooge had not given up yet.

"We'll have one more try," he said, lifting his gun. "Come on, hound. We are going to try some duck shooting. Surely, even you can retrieve duck."

"Woof! Woof!" barked Pluto happily, and off they went along the tracks towards the lake, Pluto trotting ahead sniffing the air.

Pluto thought to himself that if he tried very hard indeed he might just do it right. Then Uncle Scrooge would not think him stupid.

He walked along in front, looking all round him and trying to be very,

very good. Then, wham! he stopped dead.

"Ha!" cried Uncle Scrooge. "Seen anything?"

"Woof," barked Pluto, and Uncle Scrooge saw there was a lake full of ducks – fine, fat ducks. He hid himself in the reeds.

"At last, here are some prime ducks!" He took aim and fired, once, twice, three times. Bang! Bang! Bang!

Uncle Scrooge was very pleased.

"Hey! Whadya think you're doing?" cried a man, jumping up from the opposite bank. "You stupid numbskull! You idiot! You've just shot my decoy ducks!"

He waved his arms in rage.

"I've shot your what?" stammered Uncle Scrooge.

"My wooden decoy ducks. They make real ducks come to the lake! You owe me £10."

"Oh no!" cried Uncle Scrooge. "You wretched dog! You stupid hound! It's your fault!"

He was so mad he walked away in a hurry. His hunting was ruined, all because of a dog!

Poor Pluto. He was very sad.

Uncle Scrooge was in such a rage he didn't look where he was going and fell over a stone.

He lay there for a while groaning then he tried to get up, but it was no use. He had twisted his ankle and couldn't walk.

"Helppp!!" he yelled.

Pluto pricked up his ears. "A rescue!" he thought. "That's more like it." Off he dashed to see what was wrong.

He picked up Uncle Scrooge by his belt and carried him all the way home.

"Bravo Pluto! You're a great dog!" Uncle Scrooge said gratefully.

And Pluto went home feeling very happy, after such a disastrous day.

PLUTO'S FIVE BONES
CAN YOU FIND THEM ?

ALICE IN WONDERLAND

Among the highlights of the show is a special adaptation of Lewis Carroll's 'Alice in Wonderland'.

It opens on a huge storybook screen, where Alice and the story are introduced to the audience. The action suddenly leaps from the cartoon screen on to the arena stage where real live characters, led by Alice, follow the White Rabbit through a floral Wonderland and other magical settings.

The White Rabbit leads Alice off to join the Walrus, Tweedle Dum and Tweedle Dee, the Mad Hatter, the March Hare and the Dormouse to the un-birthday party. Alice dances with thirty-two girls dressed as flowers, and is chased by thirty-two marching cards, each over eight feet tall.

There are giant tea cups which eject their sugar lumps, spoons that stir themselves, and all other kinds of exciting tricks.

ALICE IN WONDERLAND

ALICE WAS feeling very sleepy. It really was a very hot day. She was wondering whether she should pick some daisies to make a daisy-chain when suddenly, to her great surprise, a White Rabbit with pink eyes, ran in front of her. There was nothing very strange in that but she was astonished to hear him say to himself, "Oh dear! Oh dear! I shall be too late!"

Then she could hardly believe her eyes, for the White Rabbit took a watch out of his waistcoat-pocket! He looked at it anxiously. "Oh dear! Oh dear!" he muttered. "I am in a rabbit stew! I'm late, I'm late, I'm late!"

Now Alice had never seen a rabbit with a waistcoat-pocket before, or with a watch to take out of it for that matter. So she was very, very curious. Quickly she hurried after him.

The White Rabbit hopped across

the brook and Alice was just in time to catch a glimpse of his little white tail before he disappeared into a hollow tree.

"I wonder where he's going," said Alice. "Perhaps he's off to a party. I *love* parties, so I'll go too."

So, without stopping to think how she would get out again, Alice crawled into the tree.

There was a long, dark tunnel inside. "What a strange place to give a party," she thought as she crawled along. But suddenly the tunnel dipped down. So suddenly that Alice hadn't a moment to think about stopping herself. She began to fall! Down, down, down . . . into a deep, dark well.

But the strange thing was she fell very, very slowly. It was as if she were floating. She had plenty of time to look about her. She could see cupboards and bookshelves on the sides of the well, and maps and pictures hanging on pegs.

"Well!" thought Alice. "After such a fall as this, I shall think nothing of tumbling downstairs!"

Down, down, down. Would the fall *never* come to an end? "I wonder how many miles I've fallen by this time?" she said aloud. But suddenly, thump! thump! She had landed on a heap of dry leaves.

She looked around her and was just in time to see the White Rabbit disappearing through a tiny little door. She hurried after him. As she reached the door she heard him muttering, "Oh my ears and whiskers, how late it's getting!"

Alice tried to follow him. But it was impossible. The little door led into a beautiful garden but it was much too small! Alice looked around her. There were doors all round the hall, but they were all locked. "Oh dear! Oh dear!" said Alice. "What shall I do!"

Then she saw a little three-legged table, all made of glass. There was a little bottle on it with a label tied around its neck. The words 'DRINK ME' were printed on it in large letters.

"Well, I'm not going to do that!" said Alice, who was a very sensible little girl. "It might be poison." She looked carefully at the bottle, but it was *not* marked poison. So she tasted it. It was really very nice and had a sort of mixed-up taste of cherry tart, custard, pineapple, roast turkey, toffee and hot buttered toast. And she finished it.

"What a curious feeling!" said Alice. And indeed it was. For now

she was only ten inches high! She was just about to run through the little door when she noticed a little glass box lying under the table. She opened it and saw inside a very small cake. The words 'EAT ME' were marked on it in currants. "Well, I may as well," said Alice. So she did.

To her astonishment she now saw that she was standing in the beautiful garden, but her head was high above the trees. She was more than nine feet high!

"Oh dear, oh dear!" cried Alice. "What shall I do?" Just then she noticed a little fan and a pair of white gloves lying on the ground near her feet. She picked up the fan and fanned herself with it, for growing small and then tall like this was making her feel very hot. "Dear, dear!" she said. "How queer everything is today!"

Suddenly she saw that her head was now lower than the trees. "I must be shrinking again!" she cried. "Oh dear. I hope I don't get too tiny. I might vanish altogether!"

She had almost reached her proper size when she dropped the fan she was holding. At once she stopped getting smaller. "So *that* was causing me to shrink! Oh, how nice to be my own proper size again!" she said happily.

To her great surprise, she saw that all sorts of strange animals were watching her curiously. Among

them were a Dodo, a Duck, a Mouse, and an Eaglet, and a Caterpillar smoking a long pipe. They were all very friendly and asked Alice to play a game with them.

"I would like to find the White Rabbit," said Alice. "Please, have you seen him?"

The animals tried to be as helpful as they could but they didn't know where he had gone. So Alice said goodbye to them and hurried through the gardens.

She came at last to a wood and, wandering through it, she suddenly saw a pretty little house. It had pink shutters, and on the door was a bright brass plate with the name 'W. RABBIT' on it in big letters. Suddenly the door opened and out came the White Rabbit.

He wore a beautiful uniform and looked very smart, but he still seemed very upset. "Oh, my twitching whiskers!" he said to himself, as he hurried down the garden path. "The Queen of Hearts will be so angry! Where can I have dropped them, I wonder? Oh, my dear paws! Oh, my fur and whiskers! She'll have me executed!"

Alice guessed that he was looking for the fan and gloves which she had found.

The White Rabbit had almost reached the garden gate when he caught sight of Alice.

"Why, Mary Ann, what are you doing out here?" he cried angrily. "Go inside at once and see if you

can find me a fan and some gloves. Quick, now! I'm very late!"

"But *what* are you late for?" asked Alice. "That's just what I—"

"My fan and my gloves!" said the White Rabbit firmly. "At once."

At once Alice went into the house to look for them, even though she knew she wasn't Mary Ann! "He must think I'm his housemaid," she said to herself. "What a strange little rabbit he is!"

She hurried upstairs and went into a neat little room. There was a table near the window and on it lay a fan and two pairs of tiny white gloves. She picked up the fan and a pair of the gloves and ran down the stairs again.

But when she reached the garden, the White Rabbit had disappeared once more! "Oh dear!" said Alice. "I wish he would stay still for a moment!"

So off she went again, as fast as she could, hoping to catch him up. As she was hurrying along the path through the wood, she met two little fat men.

"Hallo!" said one. "I'm Tweedledum!"

"Hallo!" said the other. "I'm Tweedledee!"

And they both grinned merrily at Alice.

"I'm Alice," she said. "And I'm looking for the White Rabbit. Which way did he go?"

"Well, if you'll have a little dance with us . . ." said Tweedledum.

"We'll tell you," said Tweedledee.

So Alice held their hands and the three of them danced round in a ring.

Tweedledum and Tweedledee were so fat that they were soon out of breath. "Four times round is enough for one dance," they said, letting go of Alice's hands.

"Well, I must get on," said Alice. "It's getting late."

"He went that way," said Tweedledum, pointing to the right.

"Just follow the path," said Tweedledee.

So, saying goodbye, Alice hurried away.

To her surprise, she came upon a table set out under a tree. The Mad Hatter and the March Hare were having tea; and sitting in the tea-pot, fast asleep, was a Dormouse. Alice was so tired that she sat down in a large arm-chair at the end of the table.

"Hallo. Have some wine," the March Hare said.

Alice looked all round the table, but there was nothing on it but tea. "I don't see any wine," she said.

"There isn't any," said the Hatter.

"Then it wasn't very polite of you to offer it," said Alice crossly.

"It wasn't very polite of you to sit down without being invited," said the March Hare.

"But there's plenty of room," said Alice.

"And you may as well have some tea now that you're here," and the Mad Hatter poured her a cup, out of another pot.

Just then the Dormouse woke up and began to tell them a story. But the Mad Hatter and the March Hare were very rude and kept on interrupting. Alice couldn't bear it any longer.

She got up angrily and walked off.

As she hurried along, Alice was startled to see a Cheshire Cat sitting on a branch of a tree. It grinned when it saw her.

"Would you tell me, please, which way I ought to go?" asked Alice.

"It depends on where you want to go," said the Cat, quite sensibly.

"I don't care where—" said Alice.

"Then it doesn't matter which way you go," said the Cat.

"—as long as I get *somewhere,*" added Alice.

"Oh, you're sure to do that," said the Cat, "if you only walk long

enough." He grinned at her, and then, suddenly—vanished!

Alice was not very surprised at this. She was getting used to queer things happening.

But suddenly the Cat appeared again. "Why don't you play croquet with the Queen of Hearts?" he asked.

"Who is *she*?" asked Alice in

surprise. But the Cat had disappeared again.

Alice went on her way and had not gone very far when she saw a very strange creature leaning against a tree.

"Who are you?" she whispered, a little frightened.

"I'm the Jabberwock," he said with a smile, for he really was quite friendly. But he didn't know where the White Rabbit was, either.

Suddenly the Cheshire Cat was back again, a big grin on his face. "There *is* a short cut," he said. "Just follow your nose."

So Alice walked on, following her nose, until she came to a little gate. She opened it and found herself back in the beautiful garden again, among the bright flower-beds and the cool fountains.

A large rose-tree stood near the gate. The roses growing on it were white, but three gardeners were busy painting them red.

"Why are you doing that?" asked Alice, a little timidly.

"Why, the fact is, Miss," said one of them, "this here ought to have been a *red* rose tree, and we put a white one in by mistake. If the Queen found out, we should all have our heads cut off!"

Just at this moment a trumpet blew a great fanfare and a voice called out, "Make way for the Queen of Hearts!"

There was a sound of many footsteps and a grand procession came

marching by. And who do you think led the way, blowing the trumpet?

It was the White Rabbit!

When the Queen saw Alice she stopped the procession and said crossly, "Who are you?"

"My name is Alice, so please your Majesty," said Alice very politely.

"Can you play croquet?" shouted the Queen.

"Why, yes!" Alice shouted back.

"Come on, then!" roared the Queen. "What are you waiting for!"

"But I can't," said Alice. "I mean, not *now*. I really think it's time I went home."

"What?" cried the Queen in a terrible temper. "If she won't play, off with her head!"

But Alice was getting a little tired of these strange things that were happening to her.

"I'm not frightened of you!" she

cried. "You're nothing but a pack of cards."

At these words, the whole pack rose up into the air and came flying down upon her. Alice gave a little scream, half of fright and half of anger. She tried to beat them off, and found herself lying on the bank . . .

Slowly Alice sat up, rubbing her eyes. She looked around her in astonishment. Why, it had all been a wonderful dream!

A PICTURE TO COLOUR

BRER BEAR AND BRER FOX

Brer Bear and Brer Fox, the well-known characters from the Uncle Remus stories, are always in hot pursuit of the 'not so stupid' Brer Rabbit.

In the following story, Brer Bear and Brer Fox decide to make a Tar Baby.

THE TAR BABY

ONE DAY Brer Fox and Brer Bear wuz sittin' round in de woods, an Brer Fox say, all to once, "I'm goin' to make a new sort of trap dat's sure to git Brer Rabbit!"

So he get some tar an set to work. He make him a Tar Baby and dress it in Brer Bear's clothes.

Dey took de Tar Baby, and dey sot him down by de side of de road. Den Brer Fox and Brer Bear, dey hid until Brer Rabbit comes along an spies de Tar Baby. "Howdy-do!" sing out Brer Rabbit.

Of course, de Tar Baby, he say nothin'. Brer Rabbit wait. Den he say, louder dan before, "Ain't you goin' to be perlite an say Howdy-do?"

De Tar Baby, he say nothin'. Now Brer Rabbit get mad. He draw back his fist, an *blip!* he hit de Tar Baby smack in de nose. But Brer Rabbit's fist stuck in de tar.

"Let go my fist!" he holler, an he draw back his other fist, and

blip! again he hit de Tar Baby. But dis fist stuck, too.

Well suh, Brer Rabbit kicked dat Tar Baby wif both behind feet. Den he ram him wid his head. By now, Brer Rabbit so stuck in de tar, he can't scarcely move at all.

Now Brer Fox and Brer Bear come outer de bushes. Dey dance round an round Brer Rabbit, laughin' and chucklin'.

"Brer Rabbit," say Brer Fox, "you been bossin' other folks round fer a long time. Now I'm de boss, an I'm goin' to roast you."

Brer Rabbit, he skeered, but he think he know how to get out of dis trouble.

"Roast me just ez hot ez you please," say Brer Rabbit, "but *please* don't fling me in dat brier-patch!"

"Hold on, Brer Fox," say Brer Bear. "It's goin' to be a lot of trouble to roast Brer Rabbit. First, we got to build a big, hot fire."

"Yes . . . dat's so," say Brer Fox. "Well, Brer Rabbit, I guess de best way is to skin you. Come on, Brer Bear, let's get started."

"Skin me," say Brer Rabbit, "pull out my ears, snatch off my legs, an chop off my tail, but please, *please,* PLEASE, Brer Fox and Brer Bear, don't fling me in dat brier-patch!"

Now Brer Bear sorter grumble. "Ah . . . pooh! It ain't goin' to be much fun to skin Brer Rabbit, 'cause he ain't skeered of bein' skinned."

"But he sure is skeered of dat brier-patch!" say Brer Fox. "An dat's just where he's goin' to go!"

Wid dat, he yank Brer Rabbit off de Tar Baby, an he fling him, *kerplunk!* . . . into de brier-patch!

Well suh, dere wuz a flutter where Brer Rabbit landed, den *"Ooo! Oow! Ouch!"* He screech an he squall. Den after a while, dere is only a weak whisper from Brer Rabbit.

Brer Fox and Brer Bear, dey listen. Den day laff an shake hands. "We got him! Brer Rabbit is dead!"

But right den, dey hear a scufflin' 'way at de other end of de brier-patch. An lo an behold, who do dey see scramblin' out but Brer Rabbit hisself, whistlin' and singin', and combin' de tar outer his mustarshes wid a piece of de brier-brush!

"Born an bred in de brier-patch, dat's me," laugh Brer Rabbit. "Told you not to fling me dere. In all de world dat's de place I love best!"

An *lippity clip,* he hop away.

So up an down dat countryside, Brer Fox an Brer Bear chase Brer Rabbit still. Maybe some day dey catch him. You reckon dey will?

MINNIE'S CAKES
CAN YOU FIND 8 things beginning with C ?
ANSWERS:-
CLOCK
CHAIR
COOKERY BOOK
CURRANTS
CUP
CAKES
COLLAR
COOKER
RECIPES

GOOFY THE MOUNTAINEER

CAN YOU NAME THESE MOUNTAINS?

ANSWERS

MATTERHORN
EVEREST
BEN NEVIS

SNOW WHITE AND THE SEVEN DWARFS

Snow White, one of the best loved Disney characters, appears with the Seven Dwarfs, and, of course, the Wicked Queen, who tempts Snow White with the poisoned apple. Everybody knows she should not eat the apple and tells her so, but she does . . . Our story tells you what happens next.

SNOW WHITE AND THE SEVEN DWARFS

Once upon a time in a far-away land, a lovely Queen sat by her window sewing. As she worked, she pricked her finger with her needle. Three drops of blood fell on the snow-white linen.

"How happy I would be if I had a little girl with lips as red as blood, skin as white as snow, and hair as black as ebony!" thought the Queen.

When spring came, her wish was granted. A little daughter was born to the Queen, and she was all her mother had desired. But the Queen's happiness was brief. Holding her lovely baby in her arms, she whispered, "Little Snow White!" and then she died.

When the lonely King married again, his new Queen was beautiful, but, alas, she was also heartless and cruel. She was jealous of all the lovely ladies of the kingdom, but most jealous of all of the lovely little Princess.

Now the Queen's most prized possession was a magic mirror. Every day she looked into it and asked:

"Mirror, mirror on the wall,
Who is the fairest of us all?"

If the mirror replied that she was fairest in the land, all was well. But if another lady was named, the Queen flew into a furious rage and had her killed.

As the years passed, Snow White grew more and more beautiful, and her sweet nature made everyone love her—everyone but the Queen.

The Queen's chief fear was that Snow White might grow to be the fairest in the land. So she banished the young Princess to the servants' quarters, made her dress in rags,

and forced her to slave from morning to night.

But while she worked, Snow White dreamed dreams of a handsome Prince who would come some day and carry her off to his castle in the clouds. And as she dusted and scrubbed—and dreamed—Snow White grew more beautiful day by day.

At last came the day the Queen had been dreading. She asked:

"Mirror, mirror on the wall,
Who is the fairest of us all?"

and the mirror replied:

"Her lips blood red, her hair like night,
Her skin like snow, her name—Snow White!"

Pale with anger, the Queen rushed from the room and called her huntsman to her.

"Take the Princess into the forest and bring me back her heart in this jewelled box," she said.

The huntsman bowed his head in grief. He had no choice but to obey the cruel Queen's commands.

Snow White had no fear of the kindly huntsman. She went happily into the forest with him. It was beautiful there among the trees, and the Princess, not knowing what was in store for her, skipped along beside the huntsman, now stopping to pick violets, now singing a happy tune.

At last the poor huntsman could bear it no longer. He fell to his knees before the Princess.

"I cannot kill you, Princess," he said, "even though it is the Queen's command. Run into the forest and hide, and never return to the castle."

Then away went the huntsman. On his way back to the castle, he killed a small animal and took its heart in the jewelled box to the wicked Queen.

Alone in the forest, Snow White wept with fright. Deeper and deeper into the woods she ran, half blinded by tears. It seemed to her that roots of trees reached up to trip her feet, that branches reached out to clutch at her dress as she passed.

At last, weak with terror, Snow White fell to the ground and lay there, sobbing her heart out.

Ever so quietly, out from burrows and nests and hollow trees, crept the little woodland animals. Bunnies and chipmunks, raccoons and squirrels gathered around to keep watch over her.

When Snow White looked up and saw them there, she smiled through her tears. At the sight of her smile, the little animals crept closer, snuggling in her lap or nestling in her arms. The birds sang their gayest melodies, and the little forest clearing was filled with joy.

"I feel ever so much better now," Snow White told her new friends. "But I still need a place to sleep."

One of the birds chirped something, and the little animals nodded in agreement. Then off flew the birds, leading the way. The rabbits, chipmunks and squirrels followed after, and Snow White came along with her arm around the neck of a gentle mother deer.

At last, through a tangle of brush, Snow White saw a tiny cottage nestling in a clearing up ahead.

"How sweet!" she cried. "It's just like a doll's house," and she clapped her hands in delight.

Skipping across a little bridge to the house, Snow White peeked in through one window pane. There seemed to be no one at home, but the sink was piled high with cups and saucers and plates which looked as though they had never been washed. Dirty little shirts and wrinkled little trousers hung over chairs, and everything was blanketed with dust.

"Maybe the children who live here have no mother," said Snow White, "and need someone to take care of them. Let's clean their house and surprise them."

So in she went, followed by her forest friends. Snow White found an old broom in the corner and swept the floor, while the little animals all did their best to help.

Then Snow White washed all the crumpled little clothes, and set a kettle of delicious soup bubbling on the hearth.

"Now," she said to the animals, "let's see what is upstairs."

Upstairs they found seven little beds in a row.

"Why, they have their names carved on them," said Snow White. "Doc, Happy, Sneezy, Dopey—such funny names for children! Grumpy, Bashful, Sleepy! My, I'm a little sleepy myself!"

Yawning, she sank down across the little beds and fell asleep. Quietly the little animals stole away, and the birds flew out the window. All was still in the little house in the forest.

"Hi ho, hi ho,
It's home from work we go—"

Seven little men came marching through the woods, singing on their way. As they came in sight of their cottage, they stopped short. Smoke was curling from the chimney, and the door was standing open!

"Look! Someone's in our house!"

"Maybe a ghost—er a goblin—er a demon!"

"I knew it," said one, with a grumpy look. "Been warning you for two hundred years something awful was about to happen!"

At last, on timid tiptoe, in they went.

"Someone's stolen our dishes," growled the grumpy one.

"No, they're hidden in the cupboard," said Happy, with a grin. "But hey! My cup's been washed! Sugar's all gone!"

At that moment a sound came from upstairs. It was Snow White yawning and turning in her sleep.

"It's up there—the goblin—er demon—er ghost!"

Shouldering their pickaxes, up the stairs they went—seven frightened little dwarfs.

Standing in a row at the foot of their beds, they stared at the sleeping Snow White.

"Wh-what is it?" whispered one.

"It's mighty purty," said another.

"Why, bless my soul, I think it's a girl!" said a third. And then Snow White woke up.

"Why, you're not children," she exclaimed. "You're little men. Let me see if I can guess your names."

And she did—Doc and Bashful, Happy, Sleepy, and Sneezy, and last of all Dopey and Grumpy, too.

"Supper is not quite ready," said Snow White. "You'll have just time to wash."

"Wash!" cried the little men with horror in their tones. They hadn't washed for oh, it seemed hundreds of years. But out they marched, when Snow White insisted. And it was worth it in the end. For such a supper they had never tasted. Nor had they ever had such an evening of fun. All the forest folk gathered around the cottage windows to watch them dance and sing.

Meanwhile, back at the castle, the huntsman had presented to the wicked Queen the box which, she thought, held Snow White's heart.

"Ah ha!" she gloated. "At last!" And down the castle corridors she hurried straight to her magic mirror.

"Now, magic mirror on the wall,
Who is the fairest one of all?"
she asked.

But the honest mirror replied:

"With the seven dwarfs will spend the night
The fairest in the land, Snow White."

Then the Queen realized that the huntsman had tricked her. She flung the jewelled box at the mirror, shattering the glass into a thousand pieces. Then, shaking with rage, the Queen hurried down to a dark cave below the palace where she worked her Black Magic.

First she disguised herself as a toothless old woman dressed in tattered rags. Then she searched her books of magic spells for a horrid spell to work on Snow White.

"What shall it be?" she muttered to herself. "The poisoned apple, the Sleeping Death? Perfect!"

In a great kettle she stirred up a poison brew. Then she dipped an apple into it—one, two, three—and the apple came out a beautiful rosy red, the most tempting apple you could hope to see.

Cackling with wicked pleasure, the Queen dropped her poisoned apple into a basket of fruit and started on her journey to the home of the seven dwarfs.

She felt certain that her plan would succeed, for the magic spell of the Sleeping Death could be broken only by Love's First Kiss, and the Queen was certain no lover would find Snow White, asleep in that great forest.

It was morning when the Queen reached the great forest, close to the dwarf's cottage. From her hiding place she saw Snow White saying good-bye to the seven little men as they marched off to work.

"Now be careful!" they warned her. "Watch out for the Queen." And Snow White promised that she would.

But when the poor, ragged old woman with a basket of apples appeared outside her window, Snow White never thought to be afraid. She gave the old woman a drink of water and spoke to her kindly.

"Thank you, my dear," the Queen cackled. "Now in return won't you have one of my beautiful apples?" And she held out to Snow White the poisoned fruit.

Snow White bit into the apple and fell down lifeless to the floor.

When the dwarfs came home, they found Snow White lying as if asleep. They built her a bed of crystal and gold in the forest. There they kept watch, night and day.

After a time a handsome Prince of a near-by kingdom heard travellers tell of the lovely Princess asleep in the forest, and he rode there to see her. At once he knew that he loved her truly, so he knelt beside her and kissed her lips.

At the touch of Love's First Kiss, Snow White awoke. There, bending over her, was the Prince of her dreams. Snow White knew that she loved him, too. She said good-bye to the dwarfs and left with her Prince and rode off to his beautiful Castle.

DUMBO

Dumbo, the little elephant that learned to fly in the 1941 Disney feature film, makes a grand appearance when his circus comes alive in DISNEY ON PARADE.

Some thirty-two clowns quickly build three rings for the costumed bears, elephants and chimps along with their trainers.

Five clown firemen join the fun moving into the audience to perform their antics with Dumbo right in the middle of it all.

Dumbo puts a finishing touch to the performance when, true to the original Walt Disney feature film, he flies high in the arena, his circus grand parade marching below.

On the next few pages you can see just what Dumbo had to go through before becoming a star of the circus.

DUMBO

It was spring—spring in the circus! Everyone was singing. Everyone was happy.

Happiest of all was Mrs. Jumbo, for in her stall in the circus train was a chubby, brand-new baby elephant. Though the other animals called the baby Dumbo, his mother loved him dearly. Even though his ears *were* big.

"All aboard!" shouted the ring-master.

After a long winter's rest, it was time to set out again on the open road.

"Toot! Toot!" whistled Casey Jones, the locomotive of the circus train.

And with a jiggety jerk and a brisk puff-puff, off sped Casey Jones!

It was dark when Casey Jones whistled and puffed into the station. Rain poured down hard, but the circus began to unload. The workmen jumped down from the freight cars.

They all helped to get the circus tent up—even Mrs. Jumbo's new baby helped.

By morning the rain had stopped, the tent was all set up, and the circus was busy getting ready for the big parade.

Then off pranced the gay procession down the main street. There were creamy-white horses, licorice-coloured seals! There were lady acrobats in pink silk tights, lions pacing in their gilded wagon-cages, elephants marching with slow, even steps.

The crowds on the pavement cheered. Then, suddenly, their eyes opened wide. They craned their necks. "Look . . . look!" they cried. "Look at that silly animal with the draggy ears! He can't be an elephant . . . he must be a clown!"

Sadly, Dumbo toddled behind his mother, with his trunk clasped to her tail. He tried to hurry along faster so he wouldn't hear the laughter, but he stumbled. He tripped over his ears. Down he splashed into a puddle of mud. Now the crowds laughed even louder. Mrs. Jumbo scowled at them. She picked Dumbo up and carried him in her trunk the rest of the way.

When the parade finally came back to the tent, Mrs. Jumbo put Dumbo in her wooden bathtub, and as she scrubbed she whispered comforting words.

A gang of noisy boys came pushing in first for the afternoon show. "We want to see the elephant—" they yelled, "the one with the sailboat ears! Look . . . there he is."

A boy grabbed one of Dumbo's ears and pulled it hard. Then he made an ugly face and stuck out his tongue.

Mrs. Jumbo couldn't stand it. She snatched the boy up with her trunk, dropped him across the rope, and spanked him, hard.

"Help!" he cried. "Help! Help!"

"What's going on here?" cried the ringmaster and snapped his whip at Mrs. Jumbo. "Tie her down!" he yelled.

Mrs. Jumbo reared on her hind legs. But soon she was behind the bars in the prison wagon with a big sign that said: "Danger! Mad Elephant! Keep Out!"

The next day, they made Dumbo into a clown. They painted his face with a foolish grin and dressed him in a baby dress. On his head they put a bonnet. They used him in the most ridiculous act in the show—a make-believe fire. He had to jump from the top of a blazing cardboard house, down into a firemen's net. The audience thought it a great joke. But Dumbo felt disgraced.

"He's a disgrace to us," the big animals agreed, and turned their backs on him.

Hidden in a pile of hay was Timothy Mouse, the smallest animal with the circus.

"They can't treat the little fellow that way," he muttered. "Not while Timothy Mouse is around."

"Hey there, little fellow!" he called to Dumbo. "Don't be afraid. I'm your friend. I want to help you."

"Say!" he went on, staring at Dumbo's ears. "Those ears are as good as wings. I'll teach you to fly!"

Quietly Dumbo and Timothy crept out of the tent to Mother Jumbo.

Dumbo told her all about the clown act, and how unhappy he was without her and about the wonderful idea Timothy had for making him a success.

Then sadly they said good-night, and Timothy and Dumbo continued on their way.

With Timothy as teacher Dumbo practised running and jumping and hopping. He tried slow and fast take-offs and standing and running jumps. He stretched out his wings and flapped them, 1-2-3-4. Then he tried the whole thing together. But hard as he tried, Dumbo could not leave the ground.

At last, almost too tired to stand, the two friends gave up and started gloomily back towards the sleeping circus.

"Don't worry, Dumbo," Timothy whispered, as he curled up on Dumbo's hat brim for a good night's sleep. "We'll have you flying yet!"

When the morning sun arose, Timothy was the first to awaken. He blinked and looked up. Just above him, four old black crows sat and stared at him.

"Why . . . why . . . " yawned Timothy, rubbing his eyes. "Where am I?"

"You're up in our tree," snapped the crows crossly. "That's where you are."

"Tree?" gasped Timothy. He looked around. Sure enough, there he was, sitting on a branch. He and Dumbo were up in a tree! The ground was far, far below. "But . . . but . . . how did we get here?" he stammered.

"How!" cackled the crows. "You and that elephant just came a-flyin' up!"

"Flying!" Timothy yelled. "Dumbo, Dumbo, wake up! Dumbo, we're up in a tree! You FLEW here!"

Slowly Dumbo opened his eyes. He glanced down. He gulped. Then he struggled to his feet. But suddenly he slipped on the smooth tree bark and fell. Down . . . down . . . down! He bounced from branch to branch, with Timothy clinging to his trunk. Plonk! They landed in a shallow pond just underneath the tree. The crows chuckled.

Timothy scrambled up out of the water and wrung out Dumbo's tail. "Dumbo," he panted. "You can fly! If you can fly when you're asleep, you can fly when you're awake. Your ears, Dumbo, they're your

fortune!" He grabbed one of Dumbo's wet ears and patted it. "You won't be a clown any more. You'll be famous . . . the only flying elephant in the whole wide world!"

And Timothy and Dumbo began all over again to practise flying.

But it wasn't easy. Time after time, Dumbo tried to take off. Time after time, he sprawled out flat on his face. Soon the crows began to feel sorry for the little fellow. When Timothy told them all the sad things that had happened to Dumbo because of his big ears, they flew down and offered to help.

One of the crows took Timothy aside. "Flying's just like swimming," he whispered. "It's just a matter of believing that you can do it." He turned and snatched a long, black feather from his tail.

"Here, take this . . . tell the baby elephant it's a magic feather. Tell him if he holds it, he can fly." The boss crow winked and flew off.

The trick worked like a charm. The very instant that Dumbo wrapped the tip of his trunk around the feather, flap . . . flap . . . flap! went his ears. Up into the air he soared like a bird! Over the tallest treetops he sailed. He glided, he dipped, he dived. Three times he circled over the heads of cheering crows. Then he headed back to the circus grounds.

Timothy shouted, "We must keep your flying a secret—a surprise for your act in this afternoon's show."

No one noticed Dumbo when he and Timothy came quietly back. It was already time for Dumbo to get into his costume. Inside the walls of a cardboard house he had to wait all through the show until fire crackled up around him.

At last Timothy leaned down and handed him the feather.

Crack! crackled the fire. The clown act was on! Flames shot up around the cardboard house. Clang! Clang! roared the clown fire-engine, rushing towards the blaze.

From the far end of the ring, a red-headed mother clown came running. "Save my baby!" she screamed. "He's on the top floor!"

The firemen brought a big net and held it out.

"Jump, my darling baby, jump!" shrieked the mother clown.

Dumbo jumped, but as he jumped the black feather slipped from his trunk and floated away. Now his magic was gone, and Dumbo plunged down like a stone.

Timothy saw the feather go. "The feather's a fake," he shouted frantically to Dumbo. "You can fly!"

Dumbo heard the shout and, doubtfully, spread his ears wide. Not two feet above the net he stopped his plunge and swooped up into the air!

A mighty gasp arose from the audience. They knew it couldn't be, but it was! Dumbo was flying!

The keepers freed Mrs. Jumbo and brought her to the tent in triumph to see her baby fly.

By evening, Dumbo was a hero from coast to coast.

Timothy became his manager, and saw to it that Dumbo got a wonderful contract with a big salary and a pension for his mother.

The circus was renamed "Dumbo's Flying Circus."

And Dumbo travelled in a special streamlined car. But best of all, he forgave everyone who had been unkind to him, for his heart was as big as his ears.

THE LOVE BUG

JIM DOUGLAS was a racing driver around San Francisco. Usually he had a big smile on his face, but on this particular day his smile had been replaced by a frown. The trouble was that Jim no longer had a car, and what good is a racing driver without a car?

When he got home to the old converted fire station which he shared with his sculptor friend, Tennessee Steinmetz, Jim asked Tennessee if he would lend him his ancient jalopy until he could buy one of his own, but was amazed when Tennessee told him that he had separated his old car into little pieces and built it into his latest sculpture!

So the only way left to Jim was to put a down payment on a second-hand car, and so began one of his wildest, weirdest adventures.

The owner of the nearest second-hand car showroom, Peter Thorndyke, had a beautiful assistant, called Carole Bennett. Not only was Carole beautiful, she was also mad keen on car racing, so Jim was delighted to tell her all about his record on the local circuit. Thorndyke had seen Jim arriving, and was looking forward to a quick sale. "Can I interest you in one of our Thorndyke Specials?" he asked Jim, pointing to a highly polished sports car in the centre of the showroom. But Jim was soon to discover that prices here were far above his limit and, much to Thorndyke's disgust, he made a hurried exit.

On the way out, Jim felt something bumping the back of his leg. He whipped round, ready to shout at a careless driver, but there was no driver, only a little white Volkswagen with no one behind the wheel. Jim stared at it, baffled, then shrugged his shoulders and made for home.

The next morning Jim was even more dumbfounded to see the same Volkswagen parked outside his front door. During the commotion that followed, when both the police and Thornduke accused Jim of stealing the car from the showroom, Jim decided that the best way to keep everybody quiet was to buy the car, even if he could hardly afford it.

Tennessee was thrilled: "Believe me, Jim, that little car has a real heart, and it's sure taken a shine to you," and he insisted on giving it a name – Herbie.

Jim thought the whole idea of a car with a heart was nonsense, but it soon became clear that Herbie was very special. He seemed to have a mind of his own, overtaking every car on the road with a roar like a jet-plane. Jim could

now race again, *and* win time after time: Herbie swept past the chequered flag before every other car for miles around.

Thorndyke felt thwarted. He determined to buy back the little Volkswagen, and each time Jim and Herbie raced to victory, he became more and more angry. But Jim wouldn't sell, so Thorndyke decided on a bit of skullduggery; he would ply Tennessee for the secret of Herbie's speed when Jim was away. But Tennessee would only say that Herbie was special because he had a heart. Frustrated, Thorndyke secretly slipped some cold coffee into Herbie's oil tank.

At the race next day, Jim was amazed and disappointed when Herbie began to cough and splutter, eventually grinding to a halt. It was Herbie's first defeat since Jim had bought him. Thorndyke saw his chance. Jim was so upset that he willingly sold Herbie on the spot for a very large sum of money, and soon afterwards bought a brand-new Lamborghini.

The effect of the coffee was short-lived, and Herbie, in perfect order again, reacted violently to being deserted by Jim. He roared off at top speed in the direction of the Golden Gate bridge.

Meanwhile Jim had found out about Thorndyke's scheming and raced after Herbie in the Lamborghini. Just as poor Herbie was about to throw himself off the bridge, Jim caught his back bumper and dragged him back.

After that Jim and Herbie were inseparable. Jim knew now that Tennessee had been right all along. Herbie did have a heart, and now he was the happiest car in San Francisco!

TANGLED STRINGS

Trace the strings to find out whose balloon has snapped from the string.

GOOFY

Goofy, Walt Disney's fumbling star, drives a vintage car on the stage in DISNEY ON PARADE.

In the following story, Goofy appears again in his old car, to join the DISNEYLAND PARADE.

DISNEYLAND PARADE

Donald Duck ran up to the gate at Disneyland.

"Hurry!" he called to his nephews. "We don't want to be late for the big parade!"

"We *are* hurrying, Uncle Donald," said Huey.

"Don't worry," said Dewey.

"They won't start without us," promised Louie.

Donald scooted through the gate and almost ran into Snow White and the seven dwarfs. They were all getting ready for the parade.

"Careful!" warned grumpy old Grumpy. "I just combed my beard, and I don't want it to get messed up."

The Mad Hatter was busily brushing his mad hat, the White Rabbit was fluffing up his white fur, and Alice was putting on a fresh pinafore.

Goofy was tinkering with his

can't wave the Mad Hatter's mad hat. I don't even have a beard like the dwarfs have."

"Who ever heard of a duck with a beard?" asked Louie.

"Just say hello to the boys and girls," said Dewey. "They'll all be glad to see you."

But Donald wasn't listening. "I know!" he cried. "When I march in the parade, I'll be carrying the biggest bunch of balloons in the world. Everyone will look at me!"

And Donald ran to Fantasyland and bought every single balloon the balloon man had.

"That *is* a big bunch of balloons," said Dewey.

"It's only a beginning!" shouted Donald, and he headed towards Main Street.

The balloon man in Main Street

goofy car to make sure it would clatter happily along in the parade.

Minnie Mouse had given Pluto the pup a nice bath, and now she was tying a bow to his collar.

Mickey Mouse had on his very best jacket, and he was practising on his big bass drum.

"Oh, dear!" said Donald. "What will *I* do in the parade? I can't beat a big drum as well as Mickey can. I can't drive Goofy's car. I

"I'll put up my long, long ladder so he can climb down," offered the fire chief.

"I have a better idea," said Mickey Mouse. He ran to the Peter Pan Ride.

"Tinkerbell!" called Mickey. "Tinkerbell, where are you?"

Tinkerbell had been taking a nap in Peter Pan's tree home. She was rather cross when Mickey woke her. She didn't say anything, since Tinkerbell never talked, but she made an angry tinkling noise.

"You've got to help Donald," said Mickey. "He bought too many balloons. He's all up in the air."

Tinkerbell understood how it was with balloons. She rubbed the sleep from her eyes, picked up her wand,

had hundreds of balloons. "I want every one," said Donald.

The man stared at the big bunch of balloons in Donald's hand. "Are you sure?" he asked.

"I'm sure," said Donald.

"All right," said the man, and he sold his balloons to Donald.

The moment Donald took hold of those balloons, he was lifted off the ground and went floating away on the breeze.

"I think," said the balloon man, "that he has too many balloons for a duck of his size."

"Let go, Uncle Donald!" shouted Huey. "Let go of the balloons!"

"I can't!" cried poor Donald. "I'll fall!"

and flew straight up to Donald.

Donald was very glad to see Tinkerbell. His arms were getting very tired holding on to those balloons.

"Please hurry!" said Donald.

Tinkerbell touched one of the balloons with her wand. Pop! went the balloon. She touched another balloon and another and another. Pop! Pop! Pop!

Donald drifted toward the ground.

But then a little bird flew up to see what all the popping was about.

"Cheep!" cheeped the bird when it saw Donald.

"Go away!" shouted Donald.

The little bird did go away, but it came back a moment later with

some straw. It must have thought Donald was a new kind of tree or perhaps a very solid cloud. It begin to build a nest on Donald's nose.

That tickled. "I'm going to sneeze!" cried Donald. "Look out below!"

"Kerchoo!" Donald did sneeze. He sneezed such a mighty sneeze that he let go of every one of his balloons.

On the ground, Minnie Mouse ran with a sofa cushion for Donald to fall on to. Goofy ran with a bucket of water for Donald to fall into. And the fire chief ran faster than anyone. He and his men ran with their big fire net.

Goofy drove his goofy car, and the Mad Hatter waved his mad hat. Minnie Mouse and Pluto the pup walked along with Alice. Snow White and the seven dwarfs marched in a straight line. Even the big bad wolf stopped chasing the three little pigs long enough to join the parade.

Donald and his nephews stayed close to Mickey and his big drum, and Donald said hello to all the boys and girls as he marched along.

"Ooof!" said Donald as he bounced into the net. "Wow!" he shouted as he bounced again.

When Donald stopped bouncing, Tinkerbell flew down and everyone cheered.

"Do you do this sort of thing often?" asked the fire chief.

"Not any more than I can help," gasped Donald.

"Now that you have both feet on the ground, we can start the parade," said Mickey Mouse.

"Hooray!" cried Huey and Dewey.

"I told you they wouldn't start without us," said Louie.

Mickey picked up his big bass drum. He whacked it as hard as he could whack it. Boom! Boom! And away they went.

Afterwards, Donald stopped the balloon man in Main Street.

"Not again!" cried the balloon man.

"This time," said Donald, "I want only *one* balloon." And he bought one.

Dewey bought one, too. So did Huey and Louie.

"Balloons are like a lot of things," Donald said happily. "They're nice, as long as you don't have too many."

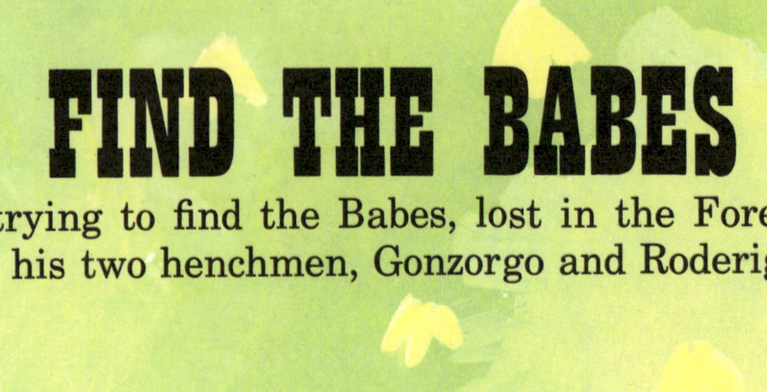

FIND THE BABES

Tom and Mary are trying to find the Babes, lost in the Forest of No Return, but wicked Barnaby and his two henchmen, Gonzorgo and Roderigo are on the look-out for them too.

Find out who gets to the Babes first by playing this game with counters and dice. One player takes the side of Tom and Mary, the other of Barnaby and his men. Throw the dice in turn and move along the squares according to the number thrown, following the instructions on the coloured squares.

1

2

3 GO AWAY! START AGAIN

4

5

6

7

DANGER 8 HURRY ON 5 PLACES

9

10

DANGER!